Aunt Patty,

Thank you for all your love and support in helping me to make this book a reality —

♡, Maureen

EXPLORING MY OPTIONS

EXPLORING MY OPTIONS

Maureen McDole

SUMMERFOLK PRESS

SAINT PETERSBURG

Copyright © 2006 by Maureen McDole

All rights reserved. No part of this book may be reproduced or transmitted in any form or by any means, electronic or mechanical, including photycopying, recording, or by an information storage and retrieval system, without permission in writing from the publisher, except by a reviewer, who may quote brief passages in a review. For information or inquiries, please contact Summerfolk Press, P.O. Box 10255, Saint Petersburg, FL 33703.

Printed and Bound in the United States of America

ISBN 0-9785004-0-7

Library of Congress Control Number: 2006904664

Design by Gabriel H. Garling

green press INITIATIVE

Summerfolk Press is committed to preserving ancient forests and natural resources. We elected to print *Exploring My Options* on 50% post consumer recycled paper, processed chlorine free. As a result, for this printing, we have saved:

- 1 Trees (40' tall and 6-8" diameter)
- 474 Gallons of Waste Water
- 191 Kilowatt Hours of Electricity
- 52 Pounds of Solid Waste
- 103 Pounds of Greenhouse Gases

Summerfolk Press made this paper choice because our printer, Thomson-Shore, Inc., is a member of Green Press Initiative, a nonprofit program dedicated to supporting authors, publishers, and suppliers in their efforts to reduce their use of fiber obtained from endangered forests.

For more information, visit www.greenpressinitiative.org

For my two grandmothers- Lorraine and Betty

Thank you for your courage, strength, wisdom and individuality.

CONTENTS

The Mermaids Gift	3
Truth or Dare?	6
Tales of a Bookworm	8
Fisherwishing	9
Wilson Was Here	10
Snook	12
Still Missing	13
No More Dolphins	15
Starfish	16
What If?	17
Hey Ladies!	19
Schools of Fish	21
It's Time	22
Should I take a Number?	24
They Forgot to Tell You	26
I Am Cold	28
Solitude	29
Staying Home	30
The Production	31
Masks	32
Holding Tight	34
Scattered	35
Listening	36

Baptism	37
Ten Dollars	38
Butter	40
Dinner Guest	41
Breaking Up	42
Prison Break	43
Growing Up	44
Exploring My Options	45
Main Objective	46
Wild Woman	47
Shedding Skins	48
Scarred	49
Saying Goodbye	50
Layers	51
I Am Female	52
I Reserve the Right	55
The Huntress	56
The Butterfly	58
Sacred Witness	60
At The Beginning	61
The Stalker	62
Directions	63
Bottomless	64
Starry Eyes	65
My Love	66
Roadblocks	67
Passion	68

Love	69
Someone to Write Home About	70
Soulmates	71
Morning	72
Crystal Ball	74
Family Values	76
Heaven	77
The Purity of Life	79
Clowns	80
Life Line	81
First Come, First Served	82
Creators	83
Tiny Seashells	84
We Are	85
No Choice	86
Survey	87
Reminder	88
The Warrior	89

EXPLORING MY OPTIONS

⌒ THE MERMAID'S GIFT

There once was a girl
who lived by the ocean.
She was shy and quiet,
for she was different,
she was born without a voice.

Every morning she would
wake to the ocean's call
and open her windows
and peer into it's watery eyes.

The dolphins would sing
to her and she would reply
by opening her mouth wide
and with all her might attempt
to sing back to them,
but no words would come.

Sadness would then circle
her heart.

One day while walking alone
along the seashore
she saw something
out of the corner of her eye
glimmer on the surface
of the water.

It was a tail!

She rubbed her eyes
and looked again and she
saw the most beautiful
mermaid with
long red hair.

The mermaid spoke,

"We have heard

your wish deep within;
I have come to give you
your voice."

The young girl wept
with happiness.

"You must promise us
three things if we are
to give you this gift.

First, you must never
use your words to
harm another.

Second, your words
shall be used
to guide people
back to themselves.

Third, you must always
be true to yourself."

The young girl nodded
her head in acceptance
as tears stained her cheeks.

"If you accept
these three things
your voice will return
to you in the morning."

The mermaid
then dove into
the waves.

That night the girl
tossed and turned.
Nightmares filled her room.
She dreamed she was
unable to keep her
promise and her voice

was taken from her forever.

She awoke full of fear
and knew she couldn't
accept the mermaid's gift;

she didn't believe
wishes can come true.

Quickly, she dressed,
to go and find
the mermaid,

but then she heard the
familiar call of the ocean.

She opened her
windows to peer into
it's watery eyes.
The dolphins sang
to her their familiar song.

Instinctively, she opened
her mouth wide
and her voice floated
out over the waves.

In singing the song
she was born knowing,
she had accepted
the mermaid's gift.

⚡ TRUTH OR DARE?

The words
hang
on the tip
of my pen,
begging me,
to drop them
on the page.

I give them
a dirty look
reminding them
of the rejection
that awaits them.

"Why bother?" I ask.

"It's so much simpler
inside that pen,
you can play Wordball
all day and night,
the world is harsh
and unforgiving;
it's safer up there," I tell them.

They stick
their tongues
out at me
and dip
their big toes
on the page.

"Truth or dare," they ask.

"You choose." I say.

"We choose truth!" They scream,
as they jump on the page.

I am relieved.

They need to express themselves.

So be it.

I am removed of any responsibility.

If I am asked,
I will say,
the words made me do it.

TALES OF A BOOKWORM

i am not a normal girl
my list of friends is short
i wear black clothes when colors are in
i always have a smart-ass retort

i don't wear ribbons or bows
or barretts in my hair
the boys all ignore me
the girls laugh and stare

my romance with books is quite simple
they were my first love affair
life has been quite harsh
my books have always played fair

i choose to stay home
while others go out at night
i read instead of socializing
my skin is ghostly white

i know i am not normal
i don't have a date for the prom
i don't get invited to parties
i spend my life in my room

my life may seem peculiar
my seclusion may seem wrong
but i know- no matter what-
with my books is where i belong

FISHERWISHING

Sometimes I think
there is no use in wishing,
still, I cast my dreams
into the heavens like fishing.

I wait with my teeth clenched
and my hands opened wide,
till so much time passes,
I feel pushed aside.

At the very last moment
when all hope is gone,
my wish is fulfilled
and I see I was wrong.

WILSON WAS HERE

My grandfather's ghost
walks slowly,
his head cradling
his faded white captain's hat.
A blue sapphire
ring on his left hand
catches the sun
as he clutches
like a lover,
a styrofoam cup
filled with black coffee,
laced with rum.

His feet walk the boardwalk,
one foot in front of the other,
red sock,
green sock,
red sock,
green sock,
for port and starboard.

These socks
were his calling card.

The buildings he
built along the boardwalk
in the seventies
are coming down soon.
They crumble in the salt air;
old age has captured them-
and him-
in a death grip.

The boats still
come through the bridge
like clockwork
and the tides
are still doing
their dance.

Yet, change is in the air.

He walks to the end
of the old wooden dock
to look at the fishing boats
he worked so hard
to fill
to pay for
to keep.

He remembers back
to his childhood
in the carnival.
It's tricks
and gimmicks
came in useful
in the fishing business.

He died a loved man
a feared man
a hated man.

Standing at the edge
of the old wooden dock,
he overlooks all that
was once his,
he thinks to himself,
wishing, he could
carve into the railing,
WILSON WAS HERE.

The tides are shifting now.
He knows
he must return
to his place of rest.
He decides to return
another day,
to oversee the progress,
though he knows
his approval
is no longer necessary.

SNOOK

The old men
dip into the glassy calm
with their lucky poles,
we wait patiently
to dodge them;
our lateral lines
extended to the tip
of the world.

We are connected
to the abyss
through the tides.

The pilings
of the wooden docks
circled us,
we dance in unison.

We were plentiful once,
frequent in our offspring;
we are fewer now,
we stay close for protection.

In the olden days
our families prospered
before we became a sport.

The old men
and their lucky poles
embrace our spirit,
we reward them
with our flesh.

The moon light overhead
highlights their victory;
it records our history.

❧ STILL MISSING: MARCH 2, 2005

In memory of Michael Costello

I call to you
from the shore...

Where are you Mikey?

Where are you!

A poetic departure-
to be a fisherman
lost at sea.

Twenty nine years old.

You left us!
You left us!

Still missing the papers say,

three days...
three weeks...
three years...

Forever.

My imagination swims
to your watery grave,

you're holding the wheel
of your 32 foot
Gulf Breeze,
searching for the Eternal Amberjack;
the Infinite Snapper.

I call to you,
dear Michael,
my cries pierce
the watery depths,

falling on deaf ears,
for you have laid eyes
on the big prize,
whose eyes, someday,
will lay upon me.

༄

Mother Ocean,
his passion for you
was so strong;
he gave his life
for your love!

I know, she says,
I know.

He is wedded to me now
and for our honeymoon all the
fish shall come to him,
since he is finally
staying in one place.

NO MORE DOLPHINS

What if there were no more dolphins?
The stewards of the deep were gone.
Pollution from the ocean killed them;
the human race left alone.

The dolphins bring us rainbows
and connect us with God on high,
our dumping in their waters
took their ability to multiply.

We think we are not harmful
poisoning our rivers and streams,
that water flows to the ocean
it's bounty feeds you and me.

If there were no more dolphins
sea turtles, starfish or sharks,
the human race would soon follow
and then the world would go dark.

✷ STARFISH

From coast
to coast,
from shore
to shore,
I moved
to recover,
to get off
the floor.

I was fractured
in two;
split in half,
I replaced
my arms,
I grew
them back.

I am
a starfish
floating along,
if you cut off
my arms
they'll grow
back strong.

WHAT IF?

Alone in my thoughts I wonder,
what if I was a beautiful princess
who was rescued one day
by a handsome prince
on a white horse.

Alone in my thoughts I wonder,
if I make love with this man
how many women has he slept with
and is he as pure
as he claims to be.

Alone in my thoughts I wonder,
is my boss is going to
make a pass at me, again
and will this be the time
I finally stand up to him.

Alone in my thoughts I wonder,
if I will make the same amount
of money as an equally educated man
or will I be underpaid in a job
I am overqualified for.

Alone in my thoughts I wonder,
about my little sister
who is being sexually harassed
in the halls of her school
by young men who claim
to not know any better.

Alone in my thoughts I wonder
about the images in the media
that claim that all women want
to do is to wash our hair
and put on makeup.

Alone in my thoughts I wonder,
how many more women must die

at the hands of their lovers or spouses;
their hushed cries echoing,
in the ears of those left behind.

Alone in my thoughts I wonder,
if there is a place where men
and women are treated equally
and one sex isn't valued
as better than the other.

Alone in my thoughts I picture,
buying my own white horse
and riding side by side
my prince as his equal
and people following
our lead.

ℰ HEY LADIES!

Hey ladies!

Why all the backbiting,
competition and abuse?

Aren't you glad
I look as good
as I do,
sound as good
as I do,
carry myself as good
as I do?

We are the feminine face
of the creator.

We are glorious in our beauty,
shining in our examples
and powerful with our words.

Yet, we steal from each other,
stab each other in the back
and rape and murder each other
with our jealousy.

For what?

To impress the men,
who love us in our natural state?

Our warm home breasts-
Our lucious behinds-
Our lovely lips-
Our cushy arms-

Where we hold our children close
Where we hold our lovers close
Where we hold the world close

Shouldn't we hold each other close?

For we are sisters
and you are only as strong
as your weakest link.

SCHOOLS OF FISH

Sometimes I wonder
if we are all
swimming
from our soul's desire

circling
one another

schools of fish

following
a leader

searching
for directions

a marker

to guide us
to our truth

so we can
locate
our reasons
for being here

❧ IT'S TIME

Do we care
about the earth?
We leave her a mess
for another day.

Do we care
about our children?
We just give their
future away.

Do we care
about our schools?
We let the funding
slip away.

Do we care
about our families?
We ignore them
while watching
television all day.

Do we care
about a woman's
right to choose?
We push our ladies away.

Do we care
about our loved ones?
We send them
to war far away.

Do we care
about our freedom?
We just listen to what
the politicians say.

Do we care
about democracy?
We sit home on election day.

Do we care
about our individuality?
We just put
our opinions away.

Do we care
about being abused?
We just give
our hope away.

Don't you think
it's time to
look at life
in a different way?

SHOULD I TAKE A NUMBER?

I wonder
how much
I would trade
for on Wall Street?

Am I worth my
weight in gold?

If I sit around
and read my
life away,
does that
make me
worth less
than someone
who works
sixty hours
a week
and makes
$100,000 dollars
a year?

Should I
follow a path
that is
more profitable,
instead
of following
my heart?

If my bank account
shows a low
balance
and my
savings is dry,
am I doomed
to live my
life always
looking over
my shoulder?

My truck
rattles and hums,
the windows
don't roll up right
and the air conditioning
is broken, but it
still runs
and gets me
where I need
to go.
Should I trade
it in
just because
a new car
looks better?

Should I work
my guts out
now to make
lots of money
to pay off
all my bills
so I can enjoy
life when
I am sixty,
or enjoy life
now working
three days a week
so I can do my art
and keep it simple?

Is there anyone
out there who
can answer
my questions?

Do I need to take
a number?

I can wait.

I have all day.

I have been waiting this long-
what's a little longer.

❧ THEY FORGOT TO TELL YOU

They forgot
to tell you
in school
how hard
it would be
to be an artist.

The world
can be cruel,
so can your mind.
Your heart
is fragile
and your
confidence
shaky.

They forgot
to tell you
that you will
go mad
for months
and not
want to go
near your tools
or talk
to anyone
about why
you are not
producing work.

Your equipment
sits like an
abandoned site
at the corner
of your studio.
Cobwebs form
and you put
locks on the door
to forget

about it.

Months pass.

Your fingers
start to itch.

They forget
to tell you
what a long
painful process
it can be,

how people
will think
you are crazy
because you
can't make up
your mind,
whether to quit forever,
or begin again.

One day,
for no particular reason,
you open the
door to your studio
and sweep it out.

You handle
your tools,
remembering,
what drew you
to them
in the first place.

You just laugh
because your
greatest gift
has returned
never to leave you again,

you hope...

ᛋ I AM COLD

              wrap
Rilke   your
Hafiz   words
Hughes   around
              me

              wrap
Dickinson your
Brooks   words
Sexton   around
              me

              wrap
Nuerda   your
Whitman words
Plath   around
              me

              wrap
Milley   your
Blake   words
Lorca   around
              me

For I am cold.

∞ SOLITUDE

I love a moment
of quiet solitude.

The only things
I can hear
are the sounds
of my thoughts
communicating;

the heavy ones
keeping me grounded
and the light ones
reminding me to fly.

℘ STAYING HOME

My well is clear
when all the
outside world
is washed away,

out of the tip
of my pen
it flows,

soaking the page.

To much time
in the outside world:

my well dries up,
my toes begin to curl,
my ears get clogged,
my hand forgets to write;

I think I am going
to stay home tonight.

❦ THE PRODUCTION

I wrote the script,
picked the costumes,
painted the set,
cast the characters,
and set the stage
for the production
of my life.

Now I don't
want to direct it,
because I know
how it ends.

MASKS

My walls are full
of masks
red, yellow, blue
and gold.

When I put
them on my face
my heart goes
from warm to cold.

I have a mask
of indifference;
I wear it when
I do not care.

I have a mask
of illusion;
I wear it when
I need to disappear.

I have a mask
of despair;
I wear it when
I lose my mind.

I have a mask
of fear;
I wear it when
I see that love is blind.

I have a mask
for my family
and a mask
for my job.

I have a mask
of cleanliness
even though I am
a slob.

I have a mask
for fitting in
even though
I know I don't.

I have a mask
for every occasion
I wear them to
stay afloat.

I wonder what's below
my masks
is it someone
I'd like
to know?

One day I hope
I'll tire of them
and decide to
close the show.

HOLDING TIGHT

Some days
I feel weird-
alone-
separate-

I walk to a different
rhythm!

I dance to a different
drum!

I get lonely.

I hold tight
to my balloon
of optimism

yet, everyone
seems to be
holding a pin.

SCATTERED

I'm scattered
like broken glass
between two states,

my childhood
and my future;

the winds of time
shuffling me,
like a deck of cards.

LISTENING

The ideas that come from my head
scare me.

The words that form on my pen
frighten me.

The dreams that erupt in my bed
engulf me.

If I allow them to dissolve,
nothing will become of me.
If I ignore them I will disappear;
it will be the death of me.

I guess I better listen.

BAPTISM

My eyes are thick
with mud,
the wipers
are broken,

I'm in denial
of my gifts.

I stumble
down my path
refusing
any help.

The road
is mine alone.

I start to cry,
surrendering
to guidance,

my fears run
down my arms
and legs,
covering
the ground below,

I am baptized;
clean.

Help is on the way.

℘ TEN DOLLARS

When I was ten
my two uncles
had a contest
to see who
could braid
my hair-
drunk.

The winner
would give me
ten dollars.

I thought
of all the things
I could buy
with ten dollars:

ice cream
stickers
gummie bears.

So I sat there
between them
as the early
morning sun

bled
through
the
thick
white
wooden
blinds

reminding me
of a prison cell.

The air
was mixed

with bubblegum
and beer,

the smell hit
my cheeks
like they were
punching bags.

Their heavy bodies
leaned into

my freckled
ten year old arms,
as their calloused hands,

wound
and tugged
and pulled

on my salt water
knotted hair.

The contest finished.

I won.

I waited to
receive my
ten dollars;

I waited
for them
to pass out.

Then I ran out
the door
to my freedom.

BUTTER

She lived in darkness
for many years,
unable to break free
from the chains
that held her heart.

They were stronger
than she was
and they kept
out her dreams.

Then one day
she realized
they were made
of butter
and if she just
turned toward
the sun,

they would
melt away.

DINNER GUEST

The invitation said six o' clock
I had responded, yes, to the RSVP.
I put on my "look at me" dress
so everyone would notice me.

I arrived and took my place,
at the seating I was assigned,
my companions were a bit above
the social ladder I liked to climb.

I began declaring my significance
through my accomplishments and deeds,
an extravagant display of, who I am,
for all the table to see.

As I scanned the buffet,
of fruits and wines galore,
in the expressions of everyone
I saw I was quite a bore.

But, I continued the monologue,
of my desires, wants and needs.
The words flew overhead
for all the guests to see.

Again, I looked upon their faces,
every shape and size and age,
to my horror, I finally realized,
I had explained myself away.

BREAKING UP

It's time
to cut
the line,
my boat
has places
to go.

It's time
to cut
the line,
I don't want
to go
so slow.

I want
to see
vast oceans;
color and scents
galore.

It's time
to cut
the line,
I don't need
to tow you
anymore.

PRISON BREAK

Do we have the courage to set our dreams free?
Can we allow them to fly for all the world to see?

We remain in cages we build around ourselves,
internally challenging our oppression,
while putting our dreams on the shelf;
to be stored for safekeeping
in a faraway place,

why do we keep our dreams
hidden for a later date?

We can shine our brightest
and realize our light,
if we just trust in the outcome
and let our dreams take flight.

❧ GROWING UP

My need
to manipulate
is waning,
my need
to dramatize
is fading,

I guess this means
I am growing up.

ℛ EXPLORING MY OPTIONS

Awake, I flow
in and out
of doubt,

molded
to follow rules
set in place,

"for my best interests."

I desire
the freedom
my dreams
show me.

My face
shines
when I sleep;

exploring my options,

before
the alarm clock sounds
and I begin
another work day.

MAIN OBJECTIVE

Weeding my garden,
clearing out my fears;
the ground is fertile,
soaked with my tears.

My roots go deep,
I reach for the sun;
my main objective,
is to just have fun.

WILD WOMAN

My bonds
to childhood
are loosening,
the strings
of guilt
around my heart
are coming free,

the rope
around my ankles
is coming undone,
my voice
is becoming me.

I feel the stirrings
of a wild woman;
the hair on my neck
is standing up.

Open fields
look so inviting,
I need a tree
to climb up.

I am becoming
a woman:
spontaneous,
loving
and free.

I am becoming
a wild woman,

I am becoming
me.

SHEDDING SKINS

I have shed
many skins
since my youth.

The skin of indifference
and anger,
the skin of fear
and unacceptability,
the skin of self-hate
and regret,
the skin of confusion
and indecision.

I have become
a butterfly
leaving behind
my cocoon.

I have embraced
the wings of belief
and trust,
the wings of joy
and acceptance,
the wings of love
and enthusiasm,
the wings of focus
and resolve.

SCARRED

With every cell
of my body
I have lived
my own life,

with the deepest
of passion
and a good deal
of strife.

I have gone
to heaven
and hell
and back;

I have something
to tell-

life isn't easy,
life is hard,

but we must try
to be open,
or permanently scarred.

❦ SAYING GOODBYE

My life seems
light right now,
for the first time
in several years.

I have dropped
other people's sadness,
I've said goodbye
to other people's fears.

I let go of responsibilities
that are not my own,
I avoid entanglements
I no longer need,

I play in my garden on weekends,
my mind no longer
has weeds.

My life seems
the perfect fit
right now,
I think I finally
have a grip,

the world seems
so much brighter now,

I've lost my need
to quit.

LAYERS

I peel off many layers
to reveal softness underneath;

a cushy sensitive woman,
with desires,
wants,
beliefs.

They change daily,
depending,
on where the wind blows.

Across the face
of the earth
they float,

to the one who knows.

❧ I AM FEMALE

Awake
Alive
Amazing

Beautiful
Bright
Brave

Cushy
Curvy
Comfortable

Dramatic
Daring
Dreamy

Enlightened
Energetic
Enchanted

Fantastic
Fun
Fabulous

Growing
Grateful
Gracious

Happy
Honest
Hilarious

Intelligent
Idealistic
Individual

Just
Jolly
Jovial

Kind
Knowledgeable
Kinky

Loving
Laughing
Loud

Marvelous
Mysterious
Mad

Noisy
Nomad
Notorious

Opinionated
Obstinate
Obvious

Particular
Pretty
Playful

Quality
Quick
Queen

Responsible
Respectful
Reckless

Strong
Sexy
Strange

Tricky
Trusting
Truthful

Useful

Unending
Unafraid

Voluptuous
Vast
Varied

Weird
Wild
Wonderful

X treme
X plorer
X pressive

Youthful
Yearning
Yes

Zealous
Zestful
Zany

I am Female

❧ I RESERVE THE RIGHT

I am
I am
I am
who I am!

And that's my right!

I also reserve the right,
to change my mind.

THE HUNTRESS

I tiptoe
through the tall
jungle grass
slowly,
crouching down
silently,
so I can observe.

I see her.

She looks like
she normally does;
her eyes ablaze
with a fiery passion,
I don't recognize
in my own.

Her clothes are worn
and tattered
after many adventures
in the jungle.

I look at her:
dirt under her fingernails,
her bracelets tarnished
and bent,
her copper hair
is knotted
and matted;
a wide smile
stretches
across her face.

The balmy sea air
surrounds us.

I look at her
feeling
behind me,

stacked high:

bills,
housecleaning,
and work.

Pounds of regret
are wound tight
in my chest.

I look at her
standing there
in the glowing
afternoon sun;
contentment
on her face.

I am the huntress
she is the hunted.

I long to be like her,

a wild creature,
impossible to tame.

THE BUTTERFLY

She started as a caterpillar,
green and yellow
with lots of black spots.

Her beady eyes reflected
everything
yet, she wanted more.

She nestled
into her cocoon;
a warm blanket
stitched with her dreams.

She rested and changed;
her armor protected her
from the elements.

She grew and changed
and grew and changed.

One day she felt ready;
the stirrings of an appearance
felt necessary.
Her blanket felt too heavy.

She wanted to breathe.
She wanted to fly.

Layer after layer
she peeled away
her cocoon.

Wing opened-
antenna stretched-
wing opened-
antenna stretched-

Ah- to be free again...
unrestrained.

She was still a caterpillar,
but now she could fly.

It was so beautiful,
she was so beautiful

and she wanted nothing more.

❧ SACRED WITNESS

My ocean had
found it's shore.

I pushed him away,
I wanted more.

Trying to control
what I cannot control.
Trying to mold
what I cannot mold.

I broke him.

I tested him
again and again,
all he wanted
was to be my friend.

I walked away
from love's expression,
every second was
a different lesson.

Now,
I am a sacred witness,
to love's experience.

I was running
from true love,
only to return
to where I started from.

AT THE BEGINNING

How wonderful
to discover yourself
no longer
wandering
searching
broken apart
after years
of heartbreak
and regret;

to show up
at the beginning
right where
you started from.

I was given
a sample
a taste
a bite
of my future
before I knew
what it meant.

I spent
hours
years
tears
to realize
what I
already knew.

THE STALKER

Do you feel it-

Love.

Tugging at your shirtstring,
tugging at your chest,
it wants you,
it needs you-

Love.

Crawling through your days,
crawling through your nights,
it crawls slowly behind you-

tugging
tugging
tugging

Do you shoo it away,
like a pest?

Or, do you embrace it,
within your chest.

❧ DIRECTIONS

How eclectic
is love,
it's shapes
and sizes;
men and women
on a journey
to the center
of things,

each on a
different path
looking for directions,
to the core
of the universe.

Their desire
to be close,
masked,
by insecurities
and a failure
to communicate.

☙ BOTTOMLESS

I poured
my heart
into you,
but you were
a pitcher
with no bottom;

my soul
flowing out
soaking the floor.

STARRY EYES

Starry starry eyes,
starry starry sky,
how deep
do you go?

Vast vast lips,
vast vast fire,
what power
do you know?

Swirling swirly hips,
swirling swirling water,
what direction
do you flow?

Wide wide arms,
wide wide earth,
hold me
so I know.

MY LOVE

He was my shepherd
I was his dove,
unchained was our devotion
flowing
in and out
of love.

Years
of reconcile.
Years
of breaking up.

He was my meal,
I was his cup.

ROADBLOCKS

I see you so available,
just out of arm's length.

Your soft mouth
beckons mine,
your heart longs
for understanding;
your words form
roadblocks.

We are separated
by stubbornness.

Oh, consider my warmth,
I will nurture you
even when we
are old and gray.

Wouldn't your fears
like to come out and play?

PASSION

Passion
Passion
Passion

where are you?

Are you buried
deep within my bones?

Am I a reflection
of you?

I look for you
everywhere;
up mountain paths,
to the ocean's shore.

Passion
Passion
Passion

I want to look
into your eyes.

I want to look
into your soul.

What do you want,
so I know what to do?

You consume me.

Do you love me
like I love you?

❧ LOVE

Seeing
Calling
Dating
Kissing

Dreaming
Telling
Wishing
Committing

Planning
Birthing
Sharing
Listening

Traveling
Growing
Aging
Dismissing

Losing
Longing
Grieving
Missing

All
This
In
The
Name
Of
Love

❧ SOMEONE TO WRITE HOME ABOUT

I met a man
who offered me
the world,
but not in furs
and diamonds.

Sweet poetry
and enlightenment,
both with the
slightest touch.

What a comfort!

Such a joy!

Momma,
I think I like this boy.

❧ SOULMATES

Twin souls
collide,

covered
in wounds,
sorrows,
experiences,

from a life
long past.

Reunited
once again,
recognizing
their other half,

they hold on
for the ride;

dancing close.

Remembering
their love,
they decide
to give it
another try,

hoping to heal
each another,

this time around.

❧ MORNING

Laying here,
after you have
left for the day,
I remember
being close
to you.

Lips touching,
tongues dancing,
twin heartbeats,
passion rapidly
pushing blood
to the tips
of my toes.

Fingers tracing
the lines
of your face.
Face to face
you and I.

Legs and arms intertwined.

Your hair
rubbing
against my cheek.
Cheek to cheek,
kissing me
all over,
we roll onto
each other.

Smooth kissing,
carressing one another.

Movements
of the universe.

We were one,

you and I.

The rhythm
of our two bodies
moved
to the music
the Gods make,

we sang
the songs
of angels
and danced
to the sounds
of the heavens.

Moments like this
are the things
people write about,
dream about,
wished for
when they
were young.

I roll over
onto your
scented pillow,
inhale you,
smile inside,
and fall back asleep.

⌘ CRYSTAL BALL

I am late.
I am scared.

The plus or minus sign
on the preganacy test
I bought for $16.99
is a crystal ball,

holding my future
within it.

My husband says
it is the most natural
thing in the world,
trying to make me feel better,

to make us both feel better.

I say,
I know,
the baby will just grow.

But, will I?

Or, like a faucet,
will I turn off,

permently hijacked,

my life that of
a hostage,
serving the needs
of my captor.

This child,
if there is one,
will grow inside me.
My body will know
what to do.

I will just wait,
as it expands
and my appetite grows.

Is this what I want
crystal ball?

Where will my writing room go
to make way for the nursery?

Will I disappear into the
flower covered bedsheets
used to keep the baby warm?

I heard there is a whole other
set of emotions set aside
for parents- are they
the same emotions reserved
for my art?

Do I have a savings account
of them stored up somewhere
in case the baby needs
to feed on my creativity?

Am I too selfish
for this?

The minus sign comes into
the window
of the crystal ball...

my fortune is cast.

FAMILY VALUES

Commitment
is married to
Joy,
who is a teacher of
Trust,
who is a lover of
Understanding,
who is neighbors with
Curiosity,
who is friends with
New Things,
who hangs out with
Different Ideas,
who shoots pool with
I Do What I Want,
who wants to date
Creativity,
who is sisters with
Commitment,
and best friends with
Joy.

HEAVEN

In heaven,
there is a wide
green park bench;
I sit with my beloved
next to me,
his head on my shoulder.

The days are sunny,
with a nice cool breeze,
just enough to take
the heat off
and tassel our hair.

In heaven,
we spend hours,
or is it seconds,
or is it years,
talking about
our life and love and art
and music and poetry.

Trees surround us,
swaying in the wind,
they tickle us, like blinds,
blowing on the window
of our hearts. We listen
to their song.

In heaven,
my beloved pets
are there and I go
to the movies
on Sundays,
with my momma
and swim in the
celestial ocean,
when I need
aqua therapy.

I don't worry about
money and there is
always food in
the refrigerator
and gas in my car,
though I prefer to
walk and dine on
chocolates alone.

In heaven,
my loved ones
never grow old
and time is abundant
and the riches
of loving
constantly reveal
themselves to me.

The background music
floats gently around
my head;
it fills the air.

I feel light and free and in love
for all eternity.

THE PURITY OF LIFE

The purity of life:
a kiss on the cheek,
smell after a summer rain,
clean hair,
your favorite song,
and a stranger's smile.

The purity of life:
the ocean's dialogue,
a young child's surprise,
reminding us of
the color of being,
our reason's for dreaming
and acceptance of ourselves.

The purity of life:
an artist's inspiration,
love's declaration,
causing me to write
this poem to you.

How much we have to celebrate,
to sing about,
to be thankful for.

The purity of life
makes the flowers bloom,
the sun shine
and gives us permission
to shine too.

✢ CLOWNS

So we joke around
like circus clowns,
each hiding
our strengths.

We want peace
but still make war
and cry while
we're asleep.

We spin like tops
and explode
with a pop,
each time
we make love.

We are here
to play,
live and die
we may,
then our spirits
float above.

❧ LIFE LINE

Life is a series
of moments
s
t
a
c
k
e
d
  one
    on
      top
        of
          the
            other.
Joinedtogether
by

one

long

silk

red

ribbon;

a_ l_i_f_e l_i_n_e

  s   t   r   e   t   c   h   i   n   g

from the heavens
to the earth.

FIRST COME
FIRST SERVED

The blazing sun
signals
the dawning
of a new day.

A time
for reflection,
each moment
brings possibilities,
a choice,
for a new direction.

Dreams are available
for the taking;

first come
first served.

CREATORS

God speaks to us softly
deep within our ears,
"You are creators
with blessings to share."

The universe
smiles at us
when our desires
are clear.
They flow from
our spirits,
the door open wide,

we each walk our own path
with God by our side.

TINY SEASHELLS

Next time your
combing
the beach
for seashells
take time
to delight
in the tiny ones.

What is the smallest
one you can find?

It is amazing
to see that moment
of inspiration
when they are becoming

a Horse Conch,
or a Cat's Paw,
or a Lightning Whelk.

We were
that small once,
just grain of sand,
a tiny seashell,
before we became

an Angel Wing,
a Venus Sunray,
a Yellow Cockle.

WE ARE

We are a piece
of infinite things.

One blade of grass,
one color of a rainbow,
one leaf on a tree
after winter has past.

We are a part
of all that is.

Our eyes reflect galaxies,
stars upon stars.
The depth of the ocean
is but the length
of our arms.

Our cells are from asteroids,
our skin is but grains of sand,

the whole universe
is on the palm
of our hand.

NO CHOICE

I sit quietly
with my back
turned to the sun.

It's rays tap
my back,
reminding me
it's my job
as a human
to shine.

It's light penetrates
my cells,
warming,
my whole being.

I try to ignore it.

It taps me again,
reminding me
I have no choice,

but to turn around
and listen
to what
it has to say.

SURVEY

Do you know how beautiful you are?
Do you?

Do you express how loving you are?
Do you?

Do you see how infinite you are?
Do you?

Do you sense how marvelous you are?
Do you?

Do you share how gifted you are?
Do you?

Do you remember how special you are?
Do you?

Do you realize how fortunate you are?
Do you?

You are part of the stars.

Do you believe me?
Do you?

A REMINDER

A waiting room.

The loadspeaker cracks
on overhead.

"Remember,
you are not alone.

The trees
support you.
The wind
supports you.
The sun
supports you.
Your legs
support you.
Your loved ones
support you.
Your heart
supports you.
The earth
supports you.
Your dreams
support you.
The air
supports you.
The sky
supports you.
Your breath
supports you.

This is just a reminder."

Silence.

ᴄ THE WARRIOR

When you hit a brick wall-
press on.

When you reach an impasse-
press on.

When you think love can't last-
press on.

When your legs are frozen in fright-
press on.

When the unknown stretches far out of sight-
press on.

When you feel weak in the knees-
press on.

When you lose the will to believe-
press on.

When you just can't muster the strength to go on-
press on
press on
press on.

Maureen McDole lives in Saint Petersburg, Florida with her husband, Gabriel Garling, an Artist, Musician and Graphic Designer.